Variety of Life

Flowers

Please visit our web site at: www.garethstevens.com
For a free color catalog describing Gareth Stevens Publishing's
list of high-quality books and multimedia programs, call
1-800-542-2595 (USA) or 1-800-387-3178 (Canada).
Gareth Stevens Publishing's fax: (414) 332-3567.

Library of Congress Cataloging-in-Publication Data

Richardson, Joy.
    Flowers / Joy Richardson. — North American ed.
      p. cm. — (Variety of life)
    Includes bibliographical references and index.
    ISBN 0-8368-4504-8 (lib. bdg.)
    1. Flowers—Juvenile literature. 2. Angiosperms—
Juvenile literature. I. Title.
QK49.R52 2005
575.6—dc22   2004056761

This North American edition first published in 2005 by
Gareth Stevens Publishing
A WRC Media Company
330 West Olive Street, Suite 100
Milwaukee, Wisconsin 53212 USA

This U.S. edition copyright © 2005 by Gareth Stevens, Inc.
Original editions copyright © 1993 and 2003 by Franklin Watts.
First published in 1993 by Franklin Watts, 96 Leonard Street,
London EC2A 4XD, England.

Franklin Watts Editors: Sarah Ridley and Sally Luck
Franklin Watts Designer: Janet Watson
Picture Research: Sarah Moule

Gareth Stevens Editor: Dorothy L. Gibbs
Gareth Stevens Designer: Kami Koenig

Picture credits: Bruce Coleman, Ltd. – cover, 3, 11, 13, 19, 21, 27;
Frank Lane Picture Agency – 7, 17, 23; Natural History Photographic
Agency – 9, 15, 25.

Printed in the United States of America

1 2 3 4 5 6 7 8 9 09 08 07 06 05

Variety of Life

Joy Richardson

Flowers

GARETH**STEVENS**
GS
P U B L I S H I N G
A WRC Media Company

Contents

Words that appear in the glossary are printed in
boldface type the first time they occur in the text.

Flowers at Work

A flower is part of a plant. Most flowers have colorful **petals**.

Flowers are everywhere in our world. People plant flowers in gardens. Wildflowers grow by themselves in forests and fields and on the banks of rivers and streams.

Flowers have a very important job to do. Most plants grow from **seeds**. Flowers make the seeds that grow into new plants.

Flowers come in all different colors, shapes, and sizes.

Buds to Blooms

New flowers grow inside **buds**. A new bud is very small.

The outside of a bud is covered with leafy **sepals**. The sepals protect the new flower growing inside the bud.

When the flower is ready to **bloom**, the sepals spread apart, and the petals of the flower spread out. The sepals do not fall off. They curl back or stay wrapped around the **base** of the flower.

A new daffodil flower is shown here in three stages (from bottom to top): 1. inside the sepals 2. pushing through the sepals 3. in full blossom outside the sepals ➤

Petal Power

Many flowers need help from insects to make seeds. Flower petals are brightly colored so insects can easily see them.

Flower petals are **designed** to make visiting easy for insects, too. The petals of snowdrops and daffodils form tube shapes, like trumpets. This shape leads an insect to the center of the flower. The flower of an orchid has a petal sticking out like a tongue for insects to land on.

The yellow and brown stripes on the petals of these irises show insects the way inside the flower. ➡

Making Pollen

Flowers make **pollen**.

Pollen comes from the **stamen** of a flower. Stamens grow inside the ring formed by the petals of the flower. The head of each stamen contains lots of dusty, yellow pollen **grains**.

A flower has a tube in the middle of it that leads down to a **seed case**. The top of the tube is called a **stigma**. The stigma sticks up above the stamens to catch pollen grains from other flowers of the same type. A stigma must catch pollen for a seed to form.

Yellow stamens and pale stigmas are sticking out of the flowers of these lilies.

Insect Visitors

Insects visit flowers looking for food.
Many flowers have a sweet liquid called
nectar. Most insects like to drink nectar.

Insects climb into flowers to search
for nectar at the base of a flower's petals.
Bees climb into flowers to collect nectar
and pollen.

Flowers also have **scents** that insects like.
The scent of honeysuckle is very strong
at night and **attracts moths**.

**Moths and butterflies have long drinking
tubes for sucking nectar out of flowers.**

From Flower
to Flower

Insects carry pollen from flower to flower.

When an insect brushes against the stamens of a flower, pollen grains stick to its body. When the insect visits another flower of the same type, some of the pollen grains may stick to the stigma of that flower. Then, a pollen grain may travel down the tube in the center of the flower into the seed case.

In the seed case, a pollen grain joins with a tiny seed to make a new seed that will grow into a new plant. The new seed has been **pollinated**.

The body of this bee is covered with sticky pollen grains.

From Flower to Fruit

When seeds have been pollinated, they begin to grow.

The flower petals have done their work. Now, they **shrivel** and fall to the ground.

The seed case keeps growing at the top of the plant's **stem**. Each type of flower makes a different kind of seed case. The seed case becomes the **fruit** of the plant.

On apple trees, an apple forms where a blossom used to be. The **pips** in the apple core are seeds that were pollinated.

Apples are the seed cases for the pips inside them. ➤

Spreading Seeds

Flower seeds need to be spread before new plants can grow.

Flowers **produce** lots of seeds to make sure that some will grow into new plants. The heads of sunflowers are packed with hundreds of seeds. Dandelion flowers make lots of seeds with fluffy white parachutes that are blown around by the wind.

Gardeners plant seeds to grow the flowers they like. Wildflowers grow by themselves from seeds that fall onto the ground.

When they are blown away by the wind, some dandelion seeds will land in new soil and grow into new dandelion plants. ➤

New Plants

Most plants bloom once a year.

Roses grow new stems each year. The new stems grow new buds. The buds turn into new flowers. Then, insects visit, the petals fall, and the seed cases **swell** with seeds beneath the old sepals. Some of these seeds will make new plants.

Some plants, such as poppies, bloom once and then die. Poppies grow quickly. After their petals fall off, their seed cases swell. Then, the seed cases harden and shake out tiny seeds.

When the poppies in this field die, their seeds will be scattered. New poppies will grow from some of the seeds next year.

Food and Water

As new plants begin to grow, their seeds crack open. Each seed pushes out a **root** and a **shoot**. Then buds form and grow to become flowers.

Green **leaves** help make the food flowers need to grow. Some flowers store food in their stems for next year. Daffodils and tulips grow from food-storing stems, which are called **bulbs**.

Water travels up to a flower through tiny tubes in the flower's stem. If the flower does not get enough water, it will **wilt**.

Every spring, daffodils grow new flowers, using the food stored in their underground bulbs.

No Petals

Some flowers are difficult to spot because they do not have petals.

All grasses have flowers. The flowers of grasses have stamens and stigmas but no sepals or petals.

Grasses do not need insects to carry their pollen. The wind blows the pollen of grasses from one plant to another. Wheat and oats can pollinate their seeds with their own pollen.

Pollen from the flowers of grasses is blown by the wind and caught by ➤ other grass flowers of the same type.

Flower Facts

There are all different kinds of flowers in the world, but they are the same in many ways.

- Most plants need flowers to make seeds.

- Most flowers need insects to help pollinate their seeds.

- Most flowers do not last very long because they do not need to. Their lovely scents, beautiful colors, and dazzling designs all help get their work done quickly.

For More Facts . . .

Books

From Seed to Sunflower. How Things Grow (series).
  Sally Morgan (Chrysalis Education)

Plants and Flowers. First-Hand Science (series).
  Lynn Huggins-Cooper (Smart Apple Media)

The Reason for a Flower. World of Nature (series).
  Ruth Heller (Putnam)

Why Do Plants Grow in Spring? What? Where?
  Why? (series). Helen Orme (Gareth Stevens)

Web Sites

The Great Plant Escape
  www.urbanext.uiuc.edu/gpe/

How Do Plants and Flowers Grow?
  www.kidport.com/Grade1/Science/HowPlantsGrow.htm

Why Do Plants Have Flowers?
  www.cnps.org/kidstuff/pollin.htm

Glossary

attracts: draws forward by offering something inviting

base: bottom or lowest point

bloom: (v) to open up or spread outward

buds: the first signs, or beginnings, of new leaves or flowers on a stem or a branch

bulbs: large buds that, when placed underground, grow to become new plants

designed: made or put together in a special way

fruit: the part of a plant that contains seeds and, often, can be eaten

grains: small, hard, sandlike bits, or particles

leaves: the green, and usually flat, parts of a plant in which food for the plant is made

moths: insects seen mainly at night and which, except for being less colorful and having larger bodies and smaller wings, look like butterflies

nectar: the sweet liquid in flowers that attracts insects

petals: the colorful, leaflike parts of a flower blossom

pips: the seeds in apples, pears, and other plump fruits

pollen: the sticky, yellow dust, or powder, that flowers need to produce seeds

pollinated: given pollen from another flower

produce: (v) to grow, make, or manufacture

root: the underground part of a plant that collects water and minerals from the soil to help the plant grow

scents: smells

seed case: the part of a plant that contains the seeds

seeds: the parts of plants that can grow into new plants and which contain the food new plants need for growing

sepals: the leaflike parts of a flower that cover the bud and protect the petals that are growing inside

shoot: the first new growth of a plant above the ground

shrivel: to shrink and become wrinkled and dried out

stamen: the part of a flower that produces pollen

stem: the part of a plant that has leaves and flowers and connects the parts above the ground to the roots growing underground

stigma: the part of a flower that catches the pollen from other flowers so that new seeds can grow

swell: (v) to puff up or bulge outward, increasing in size

wilt: to droop and become limp or weak, often as the result of not having enough food or water

Index